Table of Content

I . Addition

II . Subtraction

III . Mixed Addition and Subtraction

IV . Comparing Numbers

V . Place Value

VI . Fraction

VII . Measurement

VIII . Time

IX . Counting Money

X . Geometry

Addition

Count and Add

5 + 3 = 8

[ ] + [ ] = [ ]

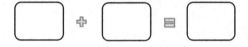

[ ] + [ ] = [ ]

[ ] + [ ] = [ ]

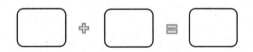

[ ] + [ ] = [ ]

[ ] + [ ] = [ ]

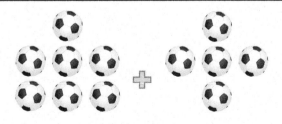

[ ] + [ ] = [ ]

[ ] + [ ] = [ ]

Count and Add

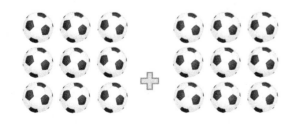

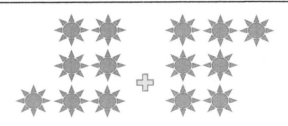

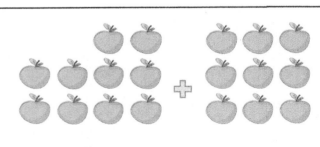

Count and Add

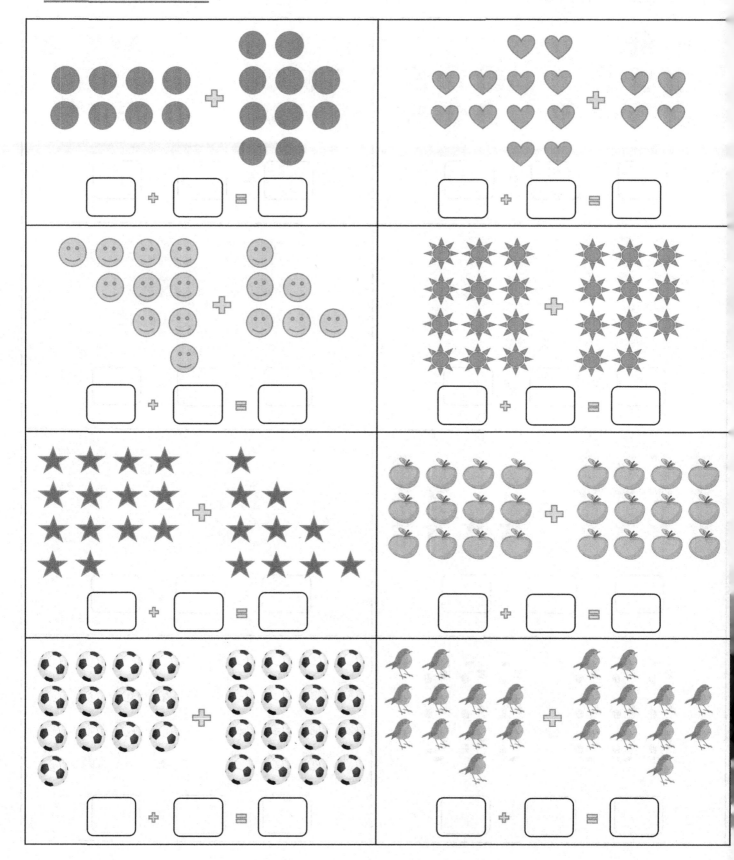

Count and Add

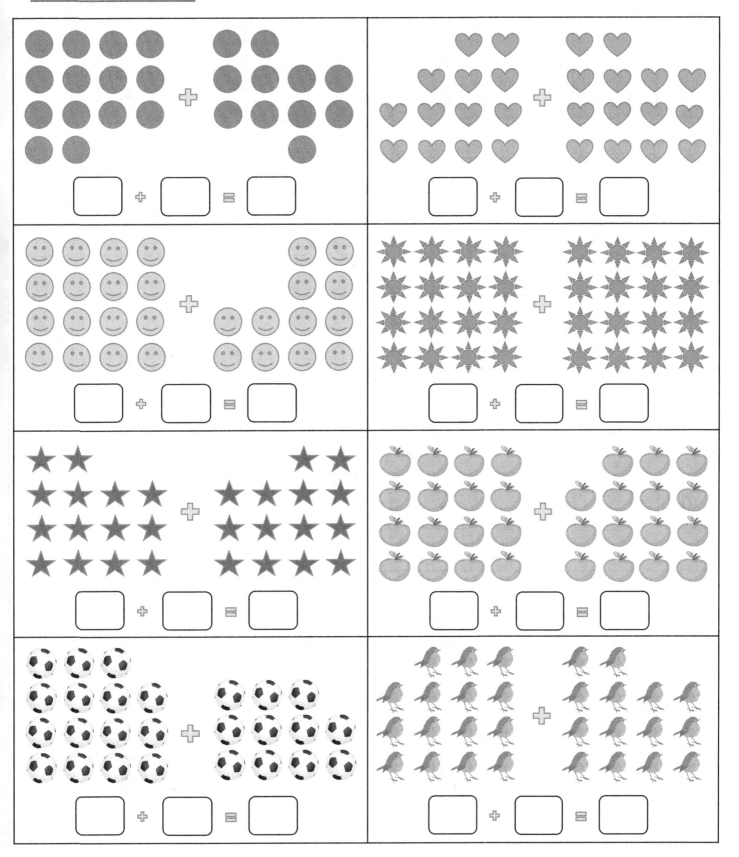

Add two numbers

Find the sums

3 + 1 = ☐	2 + 3 = ☐	4 + 5 = ☐
4 + 4 = ☐	7 + 2 = ☐	6 + 4 = ☐
1 + 6 = ☐	3 + 6 = ☐	5 + 5 = ☐
4 + 7 = ☐	8 + 5 = ☐	12 + 7 = ☐
11 + 5 = ☐	8 + 8 = ☐	2 + 18 = ☐
16 + 3 = ☐	13 + 7 = ☐	10 + 9 = ☐

Find the sums

12 + 7 = ☐	14 + 6 = ☐	14 + 5 = ☐
6 + 6 = ☐	7 + 7 = ☐	8 + 8 = ☐
15 + 5 = ☐	13 + 3 = ☐	7 + 9 = ☐
14 + 4 = ☐	8 + 9 = ☐	12 + 6 = ☐
11 + 6 = ☐	8 + 10 = ☐	1 + 18 = ☐
16 + 4 = ☐	13 + 2 = ☐	9 + 9 = ☐

Find the sums

11 + 12 = ☐	14 + 8 = ☐	13 + 9 = ☐
16 + 6 = ☐	17 + 4 = ☐	14 + 8 = ☐
17 + 5 = ☐	15 + 8 = ☐	17 + 9 = ☐
14 + 13 = ☐	20 + 9 = ☐	15 + 10 = ☐
22 + 6 = ☐	21 + 7 = ☐	25 + 5 = ☐
26 + 3 = ☐	23 + 10 = ☐	24 + 5 = ☐

Add two numbers

Find the sums

30 + 15 = ☐	27 + 19 = ☐	32 + 11 = ☐
40 + 15 = ☐	38 + 20 = ☐	25 + 17 = ☐
28 + 31 = ☐	32 + 26 = ☐	41 + 22 = ☐
40 + 33 = ☐	45 + 19 = ☐	51 + 21 = ☐
43 + 54 = ☐	38 + 62 = ☐	63 + 37 = ☐
71 + 27 = ☐	87 + 13 = ☐	92 + 8 = ☐

Find the sums

2 + 5 + 4 = ☐	7 + 3 + 8 = ☐
9 + 5 + 1 = ☐	8 + 12 + 6 = ☐
12 + 3 + 7 = ☐	15 + 4 + 3 = ☐
14 + 5 + 9 = ☐	12 + 5 + 7 = ☐
10 + 7 + 5 = ☐	17 + 2 + 8 = ☐
13 + 10 + 5 = ☐	16 + 8 + 7 = ☐
5 + 20 + 4 = ☐	10 + 10 + 10 = ☐

Find the sums

16	+	5	+	12	=			
17	+	3	+	10	=			
19	+	15	+	12	=			
18	+	12	+	16	=			
12	+	13	+	17	=			
15	+	14	+	13	=			
14	+	15	+	19	=			
20	+	15	+	17	=			
22	+	17	+	15	=			
27	+	32	+	8	=			
41	+	10	+	32	=			
36	+	28	+	17	=			
25	+	40	+	3	=			
61	+	20	+	10	=			

Find the sums

$10 + 15 + 12 = \boxed{}$	$23 + 13 + 20 = \boxed{}$
$29 + 25 + 22 = \boxed{}$	$38 + 12 + 26 = \boxed{}$
$32 + 43 + 17 = \boxed{}$	$45 + 14 + 13 = \boxed{}$
$44 + 35 + 19 = \boxed{}$	$20 + 30 + 40 = \boxed{}$
$70 + 7 + 17 = \boxed{}$	$67 + 22 + 8 = \boxed{}$
$41 + 50 + 3 = \boxed{}$	$36 + 36 + 17 = \boxed{}$
$55 + 40 + 5 = \boxed{}$	$61 + 11 + 10 = \boxed{}$

Find the sums

33 + 3	22 + 6	17 + 2	25 + 4
12 + 13	14 + 11	13 + 16	10 + 10
17 + 21	14 + 23	15 + 24	20 + 16
34 + 15	30 + 20	32 + 17	37 + 20
42 + 15	45 + 13	48 + 21	40 + 10
53 + 11	50 + 19	57 + 22	51 + 37

Find the sums

33 + 33	27 + 22	40 + 29	32 + 37
42 + 43	24 + 55	44 + 52	60 + 30
20 + 50	40 + 40	45 + 30	65 + 34
72 + 16	62 + 10	52 + 37	70 + 19
73 + 15	80 + 13	88 + 11	90 + 10
50 + 47	80 + 17	83 + 14	95 + 1

Find the sums

43 + 35	42 + 16	37 + 51	80 + 21
62 + 33	44 + 55	24 + 72	70 + 25
25 + 50	50 + 50	45 + 44	86 + 13
90 + 10	62 + 25	60 + 38	80 + 19
60 + 40	74 + 13	68 + 20	90 + 7
30 + 47	83 + 12	90 + 10	91 + 8

Fill in the missing number

2 + ☐ = 8	3 + ☐ = 10	4 + ☐ = 9
2 + ☐ = 9	3 + ☐ = 9	2 + ☐ = 7
1 + ☐ = 10	☐ + 2 = 5	☐ + 8 = 9
5 + ☐ = 13	4 + ☐ = 11	☐ + 7 = 15
☐ + 6 = 14	☐ + 4 = 17	9 + ☐ = 16
☐ + 9 = 19	10 + ☐ = 20	7 + ☐ = 12

Fill in the missing number

7 + ☐ = 20	11 + ☐ = 19	8 + ☐ = 17
11 + ☐ = 18	1 + ☐ = 20	13 + ☐ = 25
21 + ☐ = 27	3 + ☐ = 35	7 + ☐ = 39
20 + ☐ = 43	21 + ☐ = 48	30 + ☐ = 52
☐ + 2 = 57	☐ + 17 = 60	41 + ☐ = 65
☐ + 35 = 74	52 + ☐ = 79	16 + ☐ = 86

Fill in the missing number

17 + ☐ = 49	☐ + 51 = 60	20 + ☐ = 55
☐ + 31 = 77	41 + ☐ = 83	23 + ☐ = 94
11 + ☐ = 66	30 + ☐ = 70	☐ + 77 = 93
28 + ☐ = 80	36 + ☐ = 91	44 + ☐ = 99
☐ + 52 = 73	☐ + 24 = 88	53 + ☐ = 90
☐ + 45 = 96	49 + ☐ = 87	10 + ☐ = 79

To make **5 stars**, we can have

1+4 = 5 stars

2+3 = 5 stars

Now, let's think of five ways to make a group of 10 stars

☐ + ☐ = 10

☐ + ☐ = 10

☐ + ☐ = 10

☐ + ☐ = 10

☐ + ☐ = 10

To make **6 oranges**, we can have

2 + 4 = 6 oranges

3 + 3 = 6 oranges

Now, let's think of five ways to make a group of 15 oranges

| ☐ | + | ☐ | = | 15 |

| ☐ | + | ☐ | = | 15 |

| ☐ | + | ☐ | = | 15 |

| ☐ | + | ☐ | = | 15 |

| ☐ | + | ☐ | = | 15 |

To make **7 cats**, we can have

3 + 4 = 7 cats

6 + 1 = 7 cats

Now, let's think of five ways to make a group
of **22 cats**

⬜ + ⬜ = 22

⬜ + ⬜ = 22

⬜ + ⬜ = 22

⬜ + ⬜ = 22

⬜ + ⬜ = 22

To make **8 bananas**, we can have

4 + 4 = 8 bananas

5 + 3 = 8 bananas

Now, let's think of five ways to make a group of 31 bananas

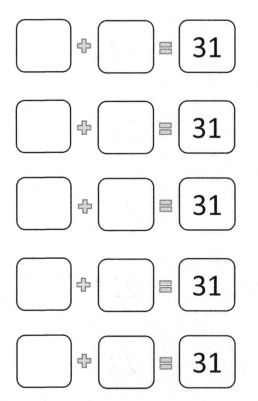

☐ + ☐ = 31

☐ + ☐ = 31

☐ + ☐ = 31

☐ + ☐ = 31

☐ + ☐ = 31

Read and solve the problems

1. Michael has five apples and William has three apples. How many apples do Michael and William have together?

_____

_____

2. Roger has ten more eggs than Catherine. Catherine has three eggs. How many eggs does Roger have?

_____

_____

3. Donald ordered 12 trumpets last week. Yesterday, he called the supplier and changed the order to add 7 more trumpets. How many trumpets did he order in total?

_____

_____

Read and solve the problems

1. Sara collects stamps. She has 21 stamps in her stamp collection book. Sara's father gives her another 14 stamps and 6 special collectible coins as her Christmas present. How many stamps in total does she has?

_____

_____

2. On the shelf, there are 17 cans of cat food and 10 cans of dog food. If James moves 9 more cans of cat food to this shelf, how many cans of cat food are there on the shelf?

_____

_____

3. Linda's hair is 23 inches long. If her hair grows 4 more inches each month, how long will it be in four more months?

_____

_____

Read and solve the problems

1. Julia has 7 apples. Jovana gave her 8 more. She needs 18 apples to make a pie. Does she have enough to make a pie?

_____

_____

2. When Sara was 12, she had 12 candles on her birthday cake. 7 girls came to her birthday party that year. This year, Sara had 8 more candles on her birthday cake. How old is Sara now?

_____

_____

3. The clown blew up 7 balloons. The other two clowns blew up ten more balloons each. How many balloons do the clowns have now?

_____

_____

Read and solve the problems

1. There are 23 first graders and 7 second graders in the first bus. In the second bus, there are 12 first graders and 15 second graders. In the third bus, there are 5 first graders and 19 second graders. How many first graders are there? How many second graders are there?

_____

_____

2. Catherine made 21 sandwiches, 13 slices of cheese pizza, 7 slices of pizza with pepperoni, 8 slices of pizza with mushroom and 2 slices of pizza with onions and olives. How many slices of pizza did she make?

_____

_____

3. There were 15 glasses of orange juice in the fridge. Diana made 7 more glasses of orange juice, 10 glasses of apple juice, 8 glasses of grapefruit juice and 5 glasses of watermelon juice. How many glasses of juice were there in total?

_____

_____

Read and solve the problems

1. Isabella is buying doggie boots for her 4 dogs. If she wants to buy them one puppy boot for each of their feet, how many boots will she buy?

_____

_____

2. Sara bought 18 bags of potato chips, 7 bags of popcorn, 5 bags of chocolate bars, 12 bags of candies and 22 bags of corn chips. How many bags of snacks did she buy?

_____

_____

3. The zoo is separated into 4 zones. The Artic zone has 6 exhibits. The African zone has 13 exhibits. The rainforest zone has 10 exhibits and the tropical zone has 20 exhibits. How many exhibits are there in the zoo?

_____

_____

Read and solve the problems

1. There are 18 staff working as cashiers and 31 staff in the kitchen. Also, there are 2 staff cleaning up the restaurant. How many staff are working in the restaurant today?

_____

_____

2. Gary played a car game at 11 a.m. The game was over after 15 minutes. he scored 61 points in first round and 32 points in second round. How many points did he have at the end of the game?

_____

_____

3. Each CD rack holds 7 CDs. A shelf can hold four racks. How many total CDs can fit on the shelf?

_____

_____

Subtraction

Count and Subtract

5 − 1 = 4

4 − 2 = ☐

7 − 3 = ☐

8 − 5 = ☐

9 − 4 = ☐

6 − 1 = ☐

10 − 7 = ☐

10 − 3 = ☐

Subtract using objects

Count and Subtract

$\boxed{} - \boxed{} = \boxed{}$

$\boxed{} - \boxed{} = \boxed{}$

$\boxed{} - \boxed{} = \boxed{}$

$\boxed{} - \boxed{} = \boxed{}$

$\boxed{} - \boxed{} = \boxed{}$

$\boxed{} - \boxed{} = \boxed{}$

$\boxed{} - \boxed{} = \boxed{}$

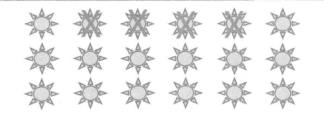

$\boxed{} - \boxed{} = \boxed{}$

Count and Subtract

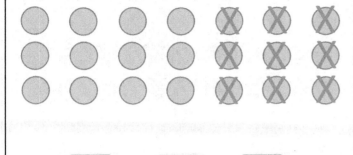

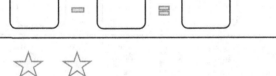

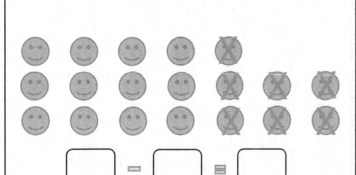

33

Count and Subtract

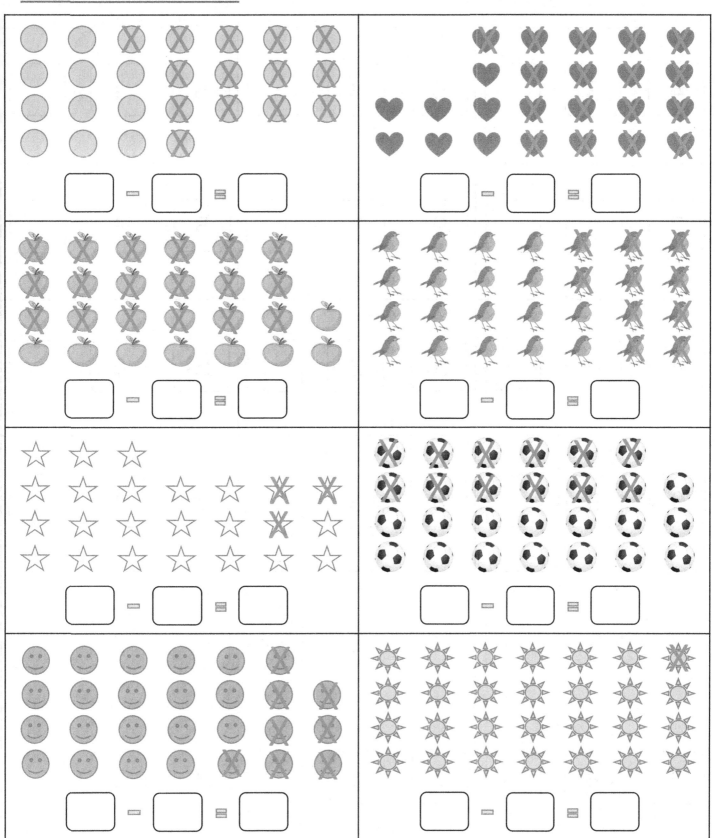

Find the difference

4 − 3 = ☐	6 − 4 = ☐	5 − 1 = ☐
7 − 2 = ☐	9 − 3 = ☐	5 − 5 = ☐
4 − 0 = ☐	10 − 3 = ☐	10 − 7 = ☐
9 − 6 = ☐	8 − 4 = ☐	9 − 1 = ☐
7 − 5 = ☐	10 − 2 = ☐	10 − 9 = ☐
9 − 8 = ☐	7 − 1 = ☐	8 − 3 = ☐

Find the difference

11 − 4 = ☐	16 − 7 = ☐	15 − 2 = ☐
17 − 2 = ☐	19 − 3 = ☐	15 − 5 = ☐
14 − 6 = ☐	13 − 3 = ☐	12 − 7 = ☐
19 − 8 = ☐	18 − 10 = ☐	19 − 11 = ☐
17 − 15 = ☐	20 − 12 = ☐	16 − 10 = ☐
19 − 18 = ☐	20 − 14 = ☐	20 − 13 = ☐

Subtract two numbers

Find the difference

21 − 6 = ☐	26 − 8 = ☐	25 − 3 = ☐
27 − 12 = ☐	29 − 13 = ☐	25 − 15 = ☐
24 − 16 = ☐	28 − 22 = ☐	29 − 20 = ☐
31 − 9 = ☐	35 − 7 = ☐	30 − 11 = ☐
37 − 15 = ☐	30 − 22 = ☐	36 − 20 = ☐
34 − 28 = ☐	39 − 24 = ☐	37 − 21 = ☐

Subtract two numbers

Find the difference

44 − 16 = ☐	46 − 8 = ☐	55 − 23 = ☐
67 − 32 = ☐	59 − 23 = ☐	65 − 15 = ☐
74 − 46 = ☐	78 − 37 = ☐	80 − 20 = ☐
61 − 9 = ☐	85 − 57 = ☐	70 − 41 = ☐
92 − 58 = ☐	96 − 10 = ☐	73 − 47 = ☐
94 − 50 = ☐	99 − 24 = ☐	88 − 66 = ☐

Find the difference

9 − 3	8 − 7	9 − 5	7 − 4
13 − 3	17 − 6	22 − 2	29 − 4
47 − 6	48 − 5	56 − 2	55 − 5
60 − 0	63 − 3	61 − 1	77 − 5
88 − 8	79 − 4	64 − 2	97 − 6
99 − 9	86 − 1	78 − 7	89 − 7

Find the difference

15 − 12	17 − 11	19 − 15	16 − 14
25 − 12	27 − 13	29 − 22	28 − 26
33 − 10	36 − 14	39 − 24	38 − 31
48 − 17	40 − 20	45 − 35	44 − 40
50 − 30	51 − 41	58 − 24	59 − 57
63 − 20	66 − 46	67 − 17	60 − 60

Find the difference

75 − 22 ─────	77 − 60 ─────	89 − 15 ─────	86 − 24 ─────
88 − 62 ─────	93 − 11 ─────	99 − 39 ─────	78 − 17 ─────
84 − 54 ─────	50 − 40 ─────	90 − 80 ─────	78 − 73 ─────
88 − 81 ─────	94 − 20 ─────	85 − 41 ─────	76 − 23 ─────
70 − 30 ─────	81 − 31 ─────	78 − 24 ─────	99 − 57 ─────
91 − 20 ─────	96 − 46 ─────	71 − 11 ─────	90 − 10 ─────

Mentalsubtraction

Fill in the missing number

7 − ☐ = 2	4 − ☐ = 1	5 − ☐ = 0
8 − ☐ = 3	6 − ☐ = 1	10 − ☐ = 8
☐ − 2 = 7	☐ − 3 = 7	1 − ☐ = 0
11 − ☐ = 4	☐ − 5 = 8	☐ − 9 = 3
18 − ☐ = 11	17 − ☐ = 1	20 − ☐ = 12
19 − ☐ = 7	20 − ☐ = 10	☐ − 10 = 9

Fill in the missing number

27 − ☐ = 2	24 − ☐ = 15	29 − ☐ = 0
38 − ☐ = 3	35 − ☐ = 31	30 − ☐ = 8
37 − ☐ = 27	40 − ☐ = 7	47 − ☐ = 21
☐ − 22 = 14	☐ − 5 = 13	☐ − 9 = 6
88 − ☐ = 11	67 − ☐ = 10	80 − ☐ = 12
79 − ☐ = 25	76 − ☐ = 28	☐ − 90 = 10

Mental subtraction

Fill in the missing number

$81 - \boxed{} = 32$ $64 - \boxed{} = 35$ $\boxed{} - 8 = 40$

$\boxed{} - 14 = 45$ $90 - \boxed{} = 51$ $\boxed{} - 12 = 67$

$\boxed{} - 37 = 57$ $89 - \boxed{} = 70$ $94 - \boxed{} = 35$

$\boxed{} - 7 = 93$ $\boxed{} - 15 = 60$ $\boxed{} - 19 = 71$

$88 - \boxed{} = 33$ $99 - \boxed{} = 90$ $80 - \boxed{} = 10$

$\boxed{} - 20 = 80$ $\boxed{} - 83 = 17$ $\boxed{} - 90 = 10$

To make **5 stars**, we can have

6 - 1 = 5 stars

9 - 4 = 5 stars

Now, let's think of five other ways to make a group of **5 stars**

☐ - ☐ = 5

☐ - ☐ = 5

☐ - ☐ = 5

☐ - ☐ = 5

☐ - ☐ = 5

To make **6 Balls**, we can have

8 - 2 = 6 Balls

Now, let's think of six other ways to make a group

of **6 Balls**

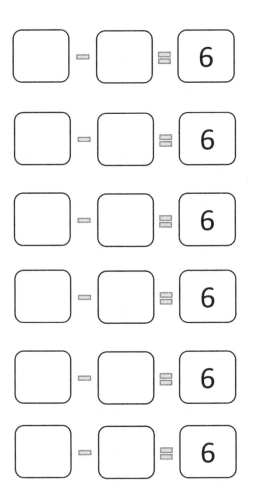

Think of six ways to make a group of **7 apples**

Read and solve the problems

1) William has 8 balls. Then William gives two balls to Michael. How many balls does William have left now?

_____

_____

2) 7 apples are on the table. Then James bumps into the table, and 3 apples fall off. How many apples are left on the table now?

_____

_____

3) James has 4 fewer pens than William. William has 9 pens. How many pens does James have?

_____

_____

Read and solve the problems

1) Farmer Michael brought 44 apples and 21 oranges to the market. He sold 16 apples. How many apples were left?

_____

_____

2) There were 56 glasses of juice. The guests at the party spilled 7 glasses of juice and drank 22 glasses of juice. How many glasses of juice were left?

_____

_____

3) There are 70 squirrels in the zoo but 18 of the squirrels are at the vet and 13 baby squirrels are in the nursery. How many squirrels are left in the squirrels cage?

_____

_____

Read and solve the problems

1) Mrs. Santiago made 77 heart cookies. She made 29 red cookies, 9 brown cookies and the rest are pink. How many pink cookies did she make?

_____

_____

2) Anita had 21 meatballs and 6 potatoes on her plate. Kirsten stole some of her meatballs. Now Anita has 13 meatballs on her plate. How many meatballs did Kirsten steal?

_____

_____

3) She ordered 28 bags of sugar, but the supplier said they can only delivery 14 bags of sugar on Friday. The rest would be delivered on Monday. How many bags of sugar will be delivered on Monday?

_____

_____

Read and solve the problems

1) He uses 40 shapes to make a picture of a robot. Sean used 10 triangles and 13 circles. How many squares did he use?

_____

_____

2) Cathy needs at least 90 points to go to level 2 in a video game. She has only 75 points in level 1. How many more points does she need to qualify for level 2?

_____

_____

3) Mrs. Franklin has 5 tulips and 49 red roses. Mrs. Snyder has 25 roses but no tulips. How many more red roses and tulips does Mrs. Franklin have than Mrs. Snyder?

_____

_____

Mixed Addition

and

Subtraction

Add and subtract

Find the solution

$6 + 5 - 3 = \boxed{}$ $4 + 3 - 5 = \boxed{}$

$9 - 2 + 3 = \boxed{}$ $8 - 5 + 1 = \boxed{}$

$2 + 7 - 8 = \boxed{}$ $10 - 1 + 4 = \boxed{}$

$6 + 6 - 6 = \boxed{}$ $10 - 8 + 7 = \boxed{}$

$9 + 9 - 1 = \boxed{}$ $10 + 3 - 9 = \boxed{}$

$3 + 10 - 4 = \boxed{}$ $7 + 6 - 8 = \boxed{}$

$5 + 10 - 7 = \boxed{}$ $9 - 1 + 6 = \boxed{}$

Find the solution

16 + 5 − 2 = ☐	14 + 3 − 15 = ☐
19 − 7 + 3 = ☐	15 − 10 + 6 = ☐
13 + 8 − 7 = ☐	11 − 8 + 5 = ☐
16 + 7 − 10 = ☐	18 − 11 + 7 = ☐
20 + 9 − 15 = ☐	19 + 3 − 18 = ☐
13 + 13 − 14 = ☐	17 + 20 − 10 = ☐
16 + 13 − 12 = ☐	12 − 1 + 16 = ☐

Read and solve the problems

1) You have 8 pieces of candy. Your mom gives you 4 more, but your brother eats 2 of them. How many pieces of candy do you have left?

_____

_____

2) Diana had 15 pennies and found 7 more. Then she gave 4 pennies to James. How many pennies did she have left?

_____

_____

3) There were 17 balls in a basket and Daniel found 8 more balls on the floor. Then, a student borrowed 6 balls. How many balls were left in the storeroom?

_____

_____

Read and solve the problems

1) Last week, the fourth graders came to the library and borrowed 23 books. This week they returned 12 books and borrowed 7 more. How many books are the fourth graders keeping at home?

_____

_____

2) 25 waiters are supposed to be at work. But 8 of them called in sick. Sara managed to call 5 extra waiters to come in to work. How many waiters are working today?

_____

_____

3) The chef used to have 20 assistants to help him in the kitchen, but he fired 7 of them yesterday and 3 of them called in sick today. How many assistants are there working in the kitchen?

_____

_____

Write the answer

6 + ☐ - 5 = 2	7 - ☐ + 2 = 6
1 - ☐ + 8 = 8	4 + 8 - ☐ = 6
5 + ☐ - 5 = 5	4 - ☐ + 4 = 8
☐ - 3 + 8 = 7	9 - ☐ + 4 = 10
11 - ☐ + 1 = 9	☐ + 17 - 3 = 14
9 + ☐ - 8 = 16	14 + ☐ - 13 = 17
11 + 8 - ☐ = 9	22 - ☐ + 3 = 12

Write the answer

$16 + \boxed{} - 5 = 25$	$17 - \boxed{} + 12 = 14$
$11 - \boxed{} + 8 = 9$	$14 + 18 - \boxed{} = 8$
$19 + \boxed{} - 4 = 22$	$24 - \boxed{} + 4 = 28$
$13 - 7 + \boxed{} = 12$	$29 - \boxed{} + 5 = 11$
$26 - \boxed{} + 2 = 3$	$\boxed{} + 30 - 3 = 31$
$32 + \boxed{} - 23 = 16$	$44 + \boxed{} - 33 = 25$
$40 + 8 - \boxed{} = 0$	$35 - \boxed{} + 1 = 31$

Comparing Numbers

Comparing Numbers

Write the correct sign < , > or =

1	<	5	7	◯	5	8	◯	6
4	◯	6	3	◯	0	2	◯	2
10	◯	9	8	◯	8	7	◯	10
11	◯	12	14	◯	20	19	◯	13
15	◯	18	20	◯	10	18	◯	3
9	◯	19	17	◯	16	19	◯	20

Write the correct sign < , > or =

30 ◯ 22	18 ◯ 35	40 ◯ 40
39 ◯ 58	16 ◯ 45	60 ◯ 50
73 ◯ 69	81 ◯ 90	7 ◯ 70
50 ◯ 23	77 ◯ 79	93 ◯ 30
55 ◯ 49	82 ◯ 84	0 ◯ 33
19 ◯ 99	100 ◯ 66	25 ◯ 70

Arrange these numbers in order, from least to greatest

Example: 1, 13, 2   1 < 2 < 13

a. 3, 9, 5	___ < ___ < ___
b. 7, 0, 10	___ < ___ < ___
c. 45, 35, 25	___ < ___ < ___
d. 30, 21, 12	___ < ___ < ___
e. 18, 39, 28	___ < ___ < ___
f. 50, 80, 79	___ < ___ < ___
g. 93, 100, 11	___ < ___ < ___
h. 99, 66, 88	___ < ___ < ___

Arrange these numbers in order, from least to greatest

a. 25, 8, 16,37   _____ < _____ < _____ < _____

b. 7, 40, 20,13   _____ < _____ < _____ < _____

c. 43, 19, 0,28   _____ < _____ < _____ < _____

d. 39, 49, 59,17   _____ < _____ < _____ < _____

e. 30, 20, 40,50   _____ < _____ < _____ < _____

f. 35, 30, 37,33   _____ < _____ < _____ < _____

g. 61, 19, 20,13   _____ < _____ < _____ < _____

h. 55, 44, 20,6   _____ < _____ < _____ < _____

i. 58, 70, 22,63   _____ < _____ < _____ < _____

j. 70, 80, 85,90   _____ < _____ < _____ < _____

k. 99, 59, 100,9   _____ < _____ < _____ < _____

l. 71, 88, 20,27   _____ < _____ < _____ < _____

m. 92, 95, 97,100   _____ < _____ < _____ < _____

n. 7, 27, 83,66   _____ < _____ < _____ < _____

o. 100, 10, 20,5   _____ < _____ < _____ < _____

p. 48, 89, 90,83   _____ < _____ < _____ < _____

Place value

Fill in the correct tens and ones for the given numbers.

4 tens and 5 ones = 45		tens and ones = 37
tens and ones = 37		tens and ones = 37
tens and ones = 37		tens and ones = 37
tens and ones = 37		tens and ones = 37
tens and ones = 37		tens and ones = 37
tens and ones = 37		tens and ones = 37
tens and ones = 37		tens and ones = 37

Fill in the correct tens and ones for the given numbers.

35	= 3 tens and 5 ones		= 2 tens and 4 ones
	= 1 ten and 0 ones		= 2 tens and 4 ones
	= 2 tens and 4 ones		= 2 tens and 4 ones
	= 2 tens and 4 ones		= 2 tens and 4 ones
	= 2 tens and 4 ones		= 2 tens and 4 ones
	= 2 tens and 4 ones		= 2 tens and 4 ones
	= 2 tens and 4 ones		= 2 tens and 4 ones

Write each number in expanded form

35 = _30 + 5_	12 = _____
27 = _____	19 = _____
52 = _____	46 = _____
69 = _____	54 = _____
77 = _____	29 = _____
91 = _____	85 = _____
88 = _____	99 = _____

Rounding

Round to the nearest ten

32 = _30_	47 = _50_
8 = _____	55 = _____
67 = _____	80 = _____
1 = _____	44 = _____
72 = _____	68 = _____
99 = _____	40 = _____
73 = _____	57 = _____

Fractions

Equal parts

Mark the shapes that have been split into equal parts:

Draw lines to divide these shapes into 2 equal parts.

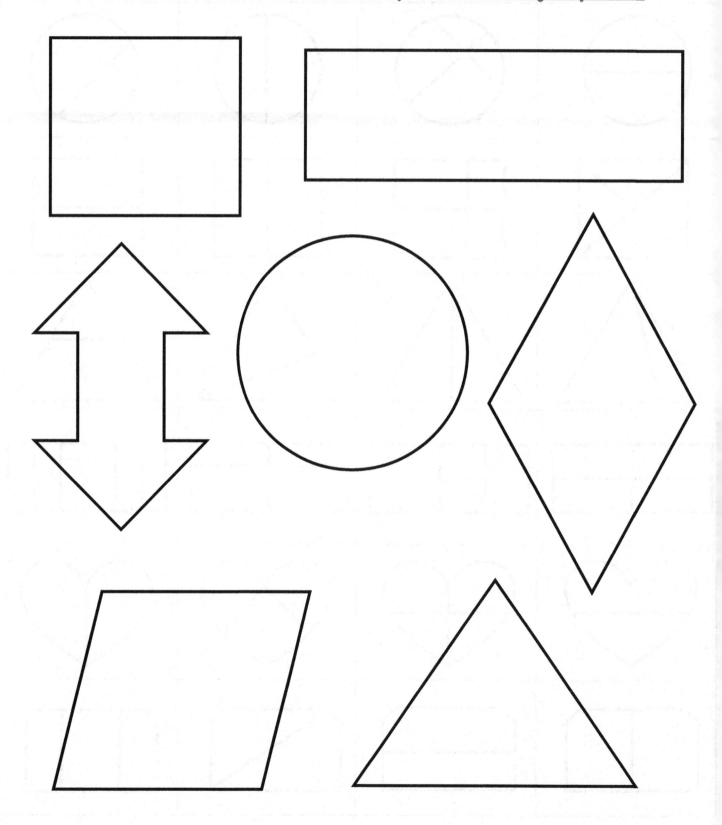

Draw lines to divide these shapes into 4 equal parts.

Draw a line to match the fraction to the words.

one half	$\frac{1}{2}$
one third	$\frac{2}{3}$
one quarter	$\frac{1}{3}$
one sixth	$\frac{1}{6}$
two thirds	$\frac{3}{4}$
three quarters	$\frac{1}{4}$
one eighth	$\frac{1}{5}$
one fifth	$\frac{1}{8}$
three sixth	$\frac{4}{4}$
four fifth	$\frac{2}{4}$
seven eighth	$\frac{8}{9}$
four quarters	$\frac{4}{5}$
eight nineth	$\frac{7}{8}$
two quarters	$\frac{3}{6}$

Coloring to make fractions

Color in the fraction shown of each shape.

 $\dfrac{1}{2}$

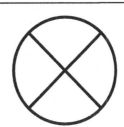 $\dfrac{3}{4}$

 $\dfrac{2}{3}$

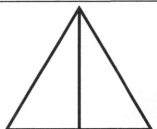 $\dfrac{2}{2}$

 $\dfrac{2}{4}$

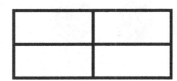 $\dfrac{1}{4}$

 $\dfrac{5}{8}$

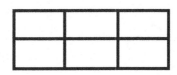 $\dfrac{4}{6}$

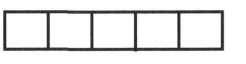 $\dfrac{3}{5}$

 $\dfrac{7}{8}$

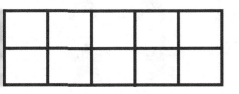 $\dfrac{9}{10}$

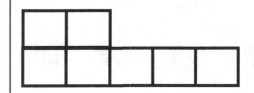 $\dfrac{4}{7}$

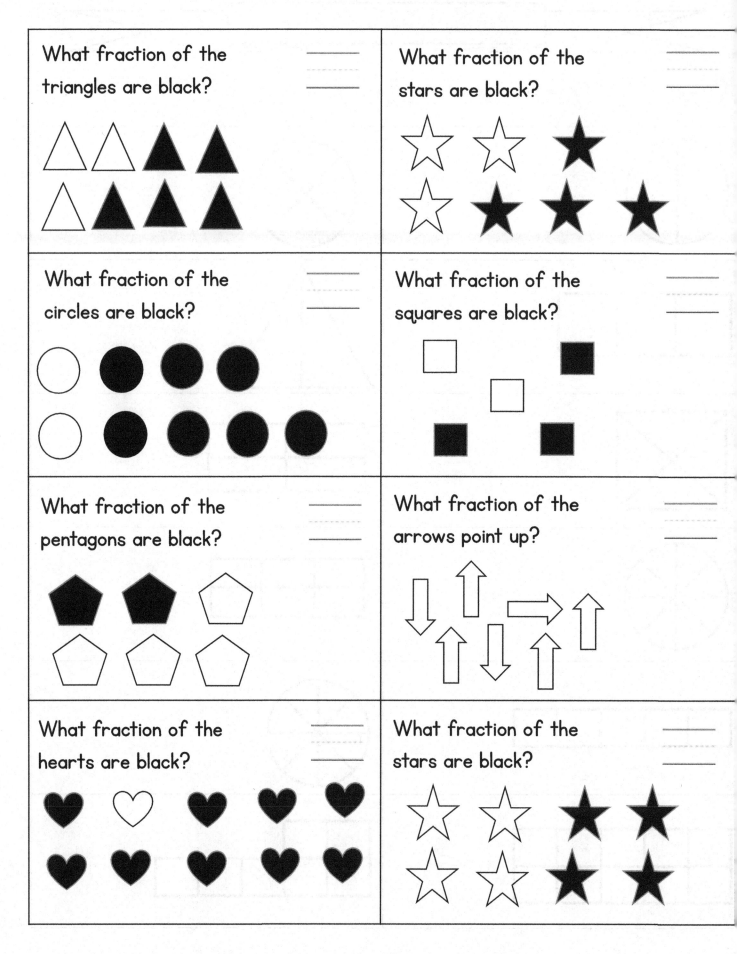

What fraction of the
triangles are black?

What fraction of the
stars are black?

What fraction of the
circles are black?

What fraction of the
squares are black?

What fraction of the
pentagons are black?

What fraction of the
arrows point up?

What fraction of the
hearts are black?

What fraction of the
stars are black?

Read and answer each question.

There are 12 buses in the parking lot. 3 buses are parked on the left and the other cars are parked on the right.

1. What fraction of the buses are parked on the right?

2. If 5 buses are black, what fraction of the buses are black?

3. If 3 buses are green, what fraction of the buses are green?

4. If $\frac{6}{12}$ of the buses are mini, how many mini are there?

5. During lunch time, $\frac{4}{12}$ of the buses left the parking lot. How many buses are left?

Read and answer each question.

There are 22 students in a class. 9 of them are girls.

1. What fraction of the class are girls?

2. What fraction of the class are boys?

3. If 13 students ordered orange juice, what fraction of the class ordered orange juice?

4. If $\frac{6}{22}$ of students brings pizza for lunch, how many students have pizza for lunch?

5. $\frac{18}{22}$ of the students bring their parent consent forms for their field trip. How many of the students have not brought in their forms?

Measurement

Wich of these objects is long , longer and longest?

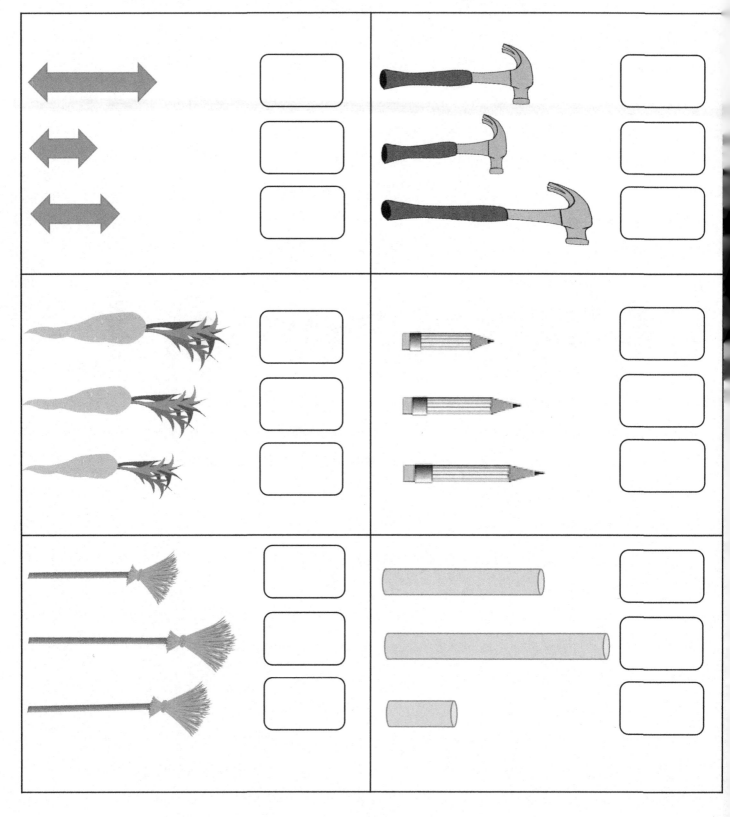

Use a ruler to measure this objects

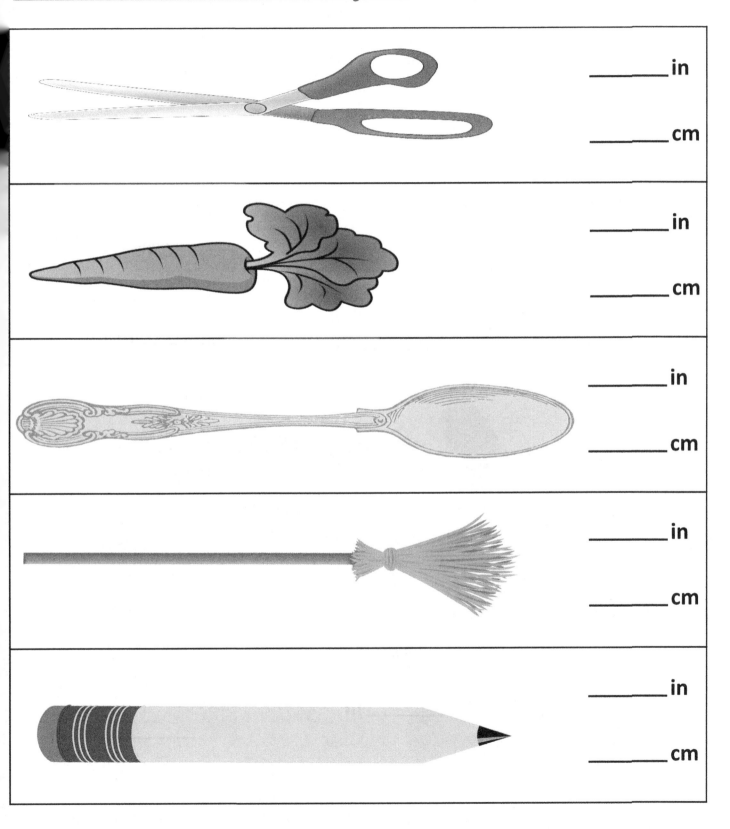

_____ in	
_____ cm	
_____ in	
_____ cm	
_____ in	
_____ cm	
_____ in	
_____ cm	
_____ in	
_____ cm	

Use a ruler to measure this objects

_____ in

_____ cm

_____ in

_____ cm

_____ cm

_____ in

_____ in

Read and solve the problems

1) Jacob's ruler is 8 inches long and Sean's ruler is 6 inches long. Who has a longer ruler?

_____

_____

2) There are 3 tubes of paint. The blue one is 7 inches long. The red one is 5 inches long and the yellow one is 9 inches long. Compared to the blue one, how much longer is the yellow one?

_____

_____

3) There are two glue sticks. The longer one is 15 cm long. The shorter one is 9 cm shorter. How long is the shorter glue stick?

_____

_____

4) The yellow crayon is used up more than the grey crayon. The grey crayon is 8 cm longer than the yellow crayon. If the yellow crayon is 3 cm long, how long is the grey crayon?

_____

_____

Circle the correct word

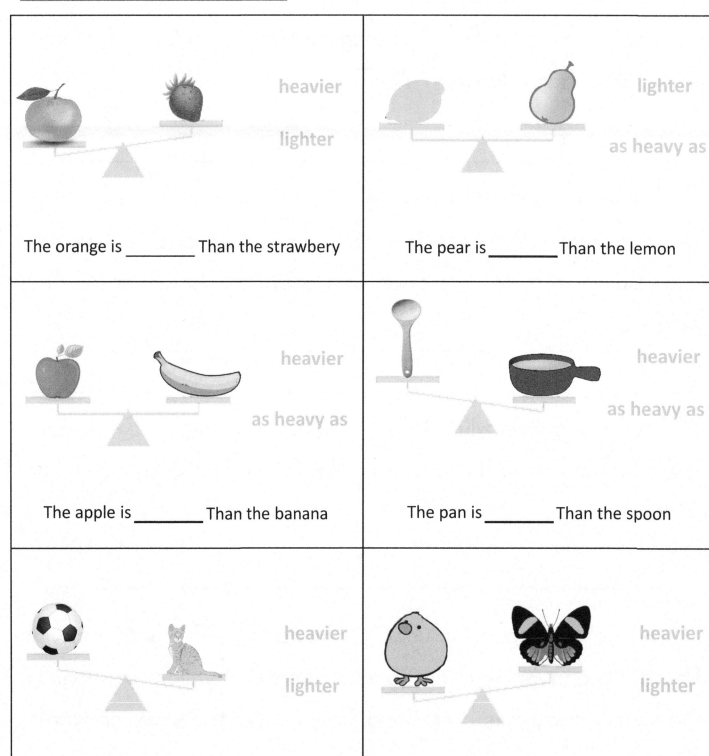

heavier

lighter

The orange is _____ Than the strawbery

lighter

as heavy as

The pear is _____ Than the lemon

heavier

as heavy as

The apple is _____ Than the banana

heavier

as heavy as

The pan is _____ Than the spoon

heavier

lighter

The ball is _____ Than the cat

heavier

lighter

The butterfly is _____ Than the bird

Color the heaviest animal

Color the lightest apple

Color the heaviest car

Color the object that is not the heaviest and not the lightest

Time

Write the time below each clock.

1.

2.

3.

4.

5.

6.

7.

8.

9.

10.

11.

12.

Draw the time shown on each clock.

1.

2.

3.

4.

5.

6.

7.

8.

9.

10.

11.

12.

Draw the time shown on each clock.

1.

| 4:00 |

2.

| 1:25 |

3.

| 8:30 |

4.

| 7:00 |

5.

| 3:30 |

6.

| 9:15 |

7.

| 9:20 |

8.

| 2:00 |

9.

| 11:5 |

10.

| 8:10 |

11.

| 6:15 |

12.

| 4:30 |

Draw the time shown on each clock.

1.

| 10:00 |

2.

| 11:15 |

3.

| 5:30 |

4.

| 7:45 |

5.

| 3:25 |

6.

| 12:00 |

7.

| 8:20 |

8.

| 1:40 |

9.

| 11:50 |

10.

| 8:35 |

11.

| 5:55 |

12.

| 6:5 |

Read and solve the problems

1) School starts at 8 o'clock in the morning and ends after 6 hours. What time does school end?

_____

_____

2) The train to Paris was scheduled to leave London at 8 o'clock in the morning, but it was delayed for one hour. If the trip usually takes about 2 hours, when will the train arrive in Paris?

_____

_____

3) The library only opens for 5 hours on Sundays. If it opens at 12 o'clock at noon, at what time does it close?

_____

_____

4) The pharmacy usually opens at 7 o'clock in the morning. However, due to power failure, it opened 5 hours later than usual on yesterday. What time was it open?

_____

_____

Counting Money

Draw a line to match the coin with its name.

Nickel

Penny

Dime

Quarter

1 Dollar

Draw a line to match the coin with its value.

5¢

10¢

1¢

25¢

1$

Add the coins.

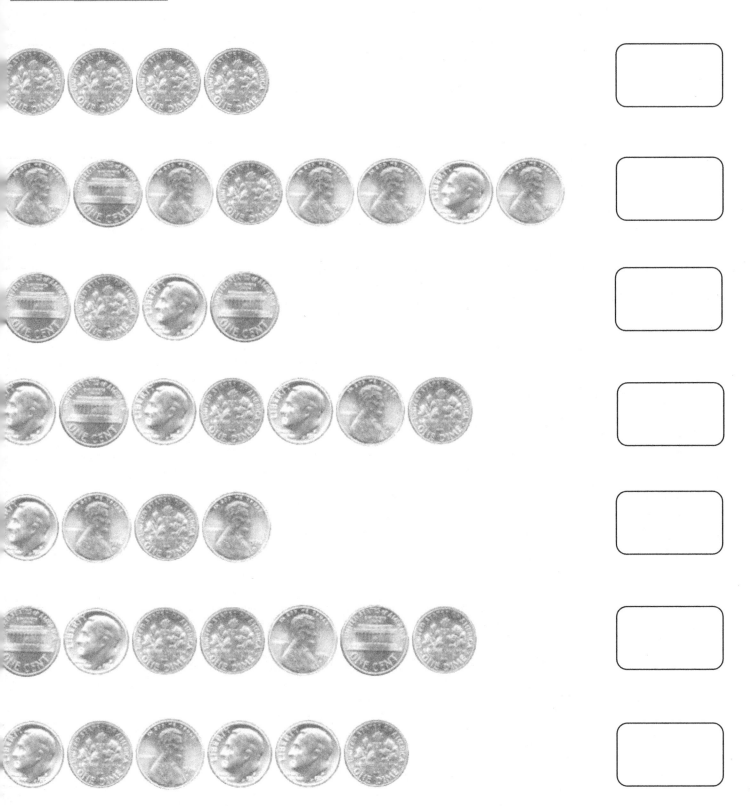

Add the coins.

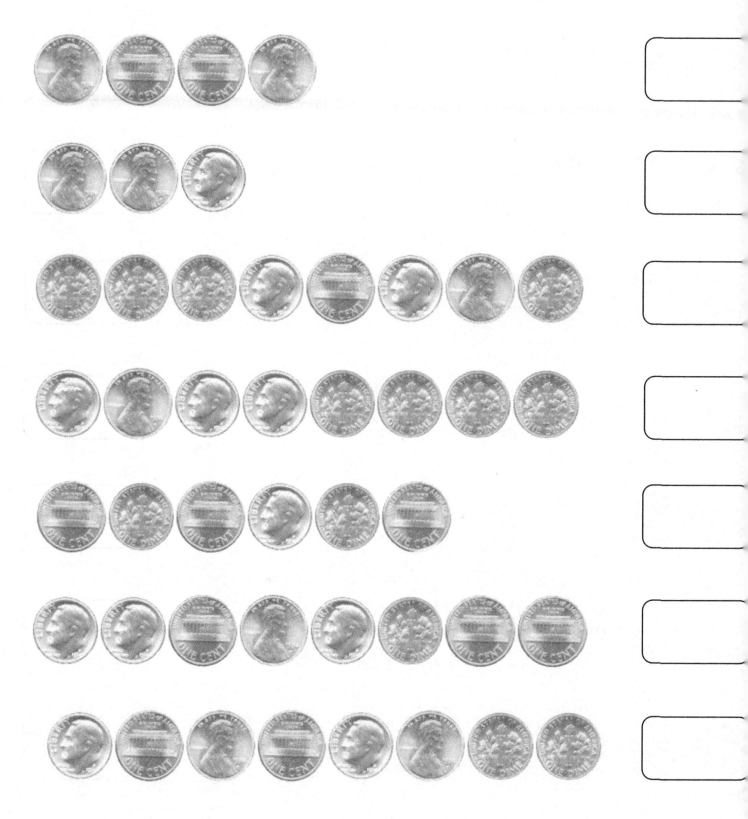

Add the coins.

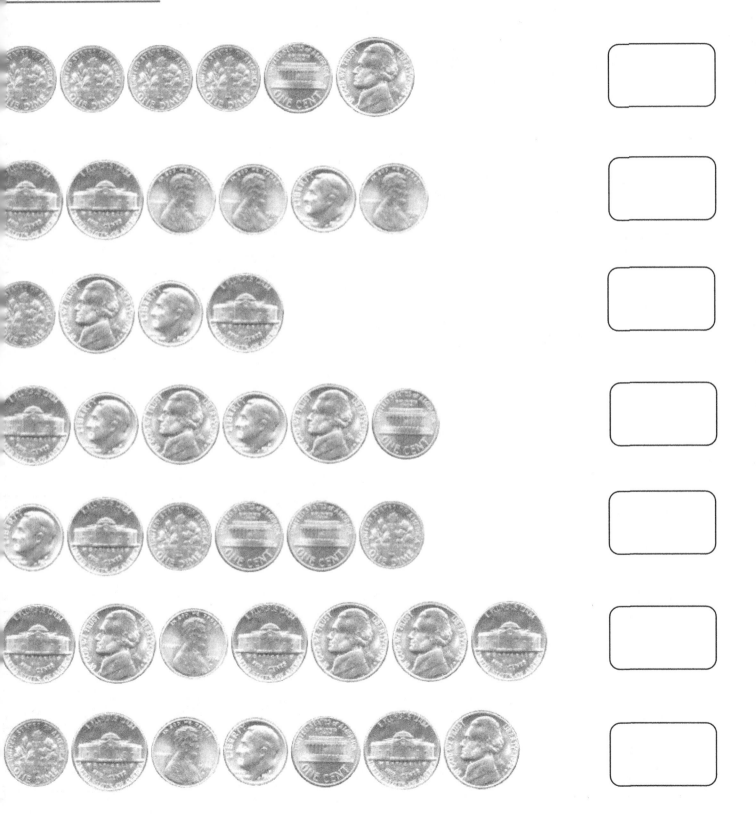

Add the coins.

Add the coins.

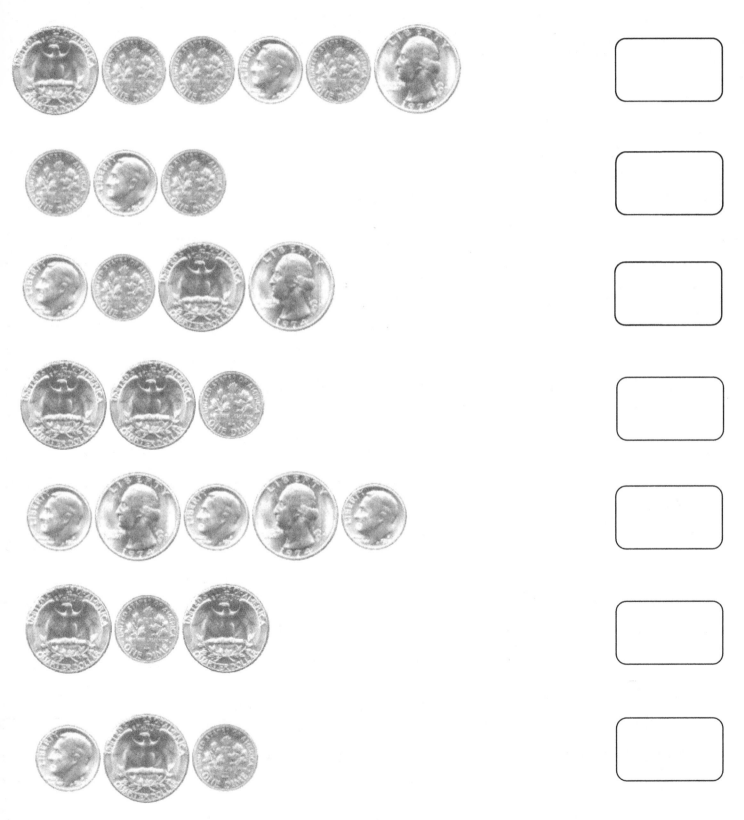

Add the coins.

Add the coins.

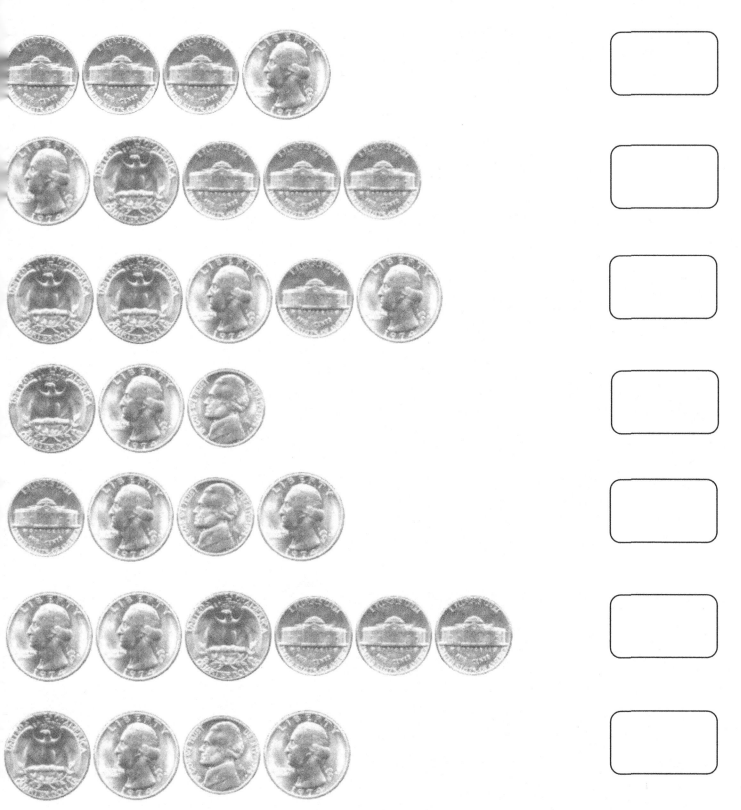

Add the coins.

Add the coins.

Add the coins.

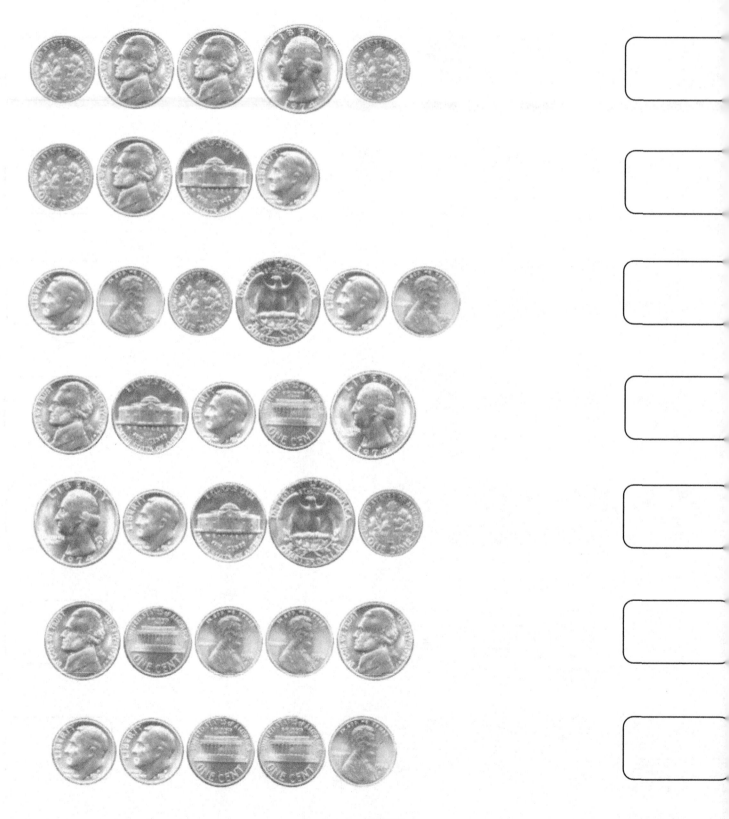

Geometry

Draw a line between a shape and its name.

	Square
	Circle
	Triangle
	Rectangle
	Cylinder
	Oval

Color all the:

a) cube red

b) cone blue

c) rectangle green

d) triangle orange

e) cylinder brown

f) Parallelogram pink

g) Rhombus

h) Trapezium purple

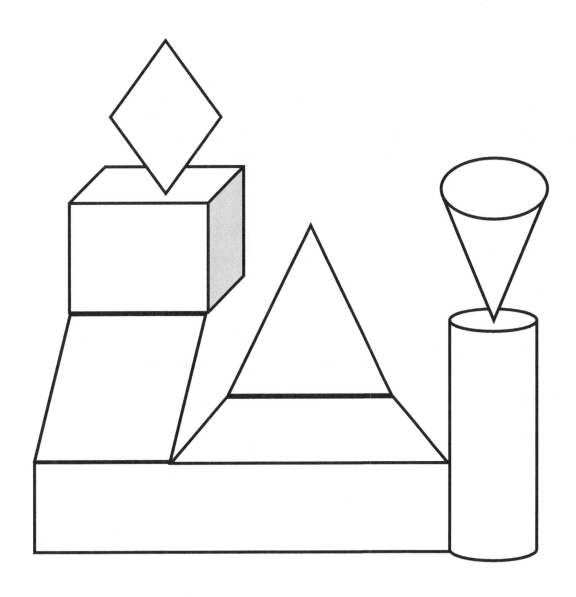

Draw the shape indicated.

Square	Triangle
Rectangle	Circle
Cylinder	Cube

Draw the shape indicated.

oval	Pentagon
Trapezium	Parallelogram
Rhombus	cone

Made in the USA
Coppell, TX
05 November 2024

39673454R00063